For Patsy!
Love + Prayers —
Always "Joy"fully
Yours —

A Mother's

PRECIOUS MOMENTS™

Verses by **Joy Morgan Davis**

Illustrations by **Samuel J. Butcher**

Fleming H. Revell
A Division of Baker Book House
Grand Rapids, Michigan 49516

Published by Fleming H. Revell
a division of Baker Book House Company
P.O. Box 6287, Grand Rapids, MI 49516-6287

Printed in the United States of America

Library of Congress Cataloging-in-Publication Data

Davis, Joy Morgan.
    A mother's precious moments / Joy Morgan Davis ; illustrations by
Samuel J. Butcher.
       p.   cm.
    ISBN 0-8007-7153-2
    1. Mother and child—Poetry. 2. Motherhood—Poetry. 3. Mothers—
Poetry. I. Butcher, Samuel J. (Samuel John), 1939– . II. Title.
PS3554.A9349126M68   1996
811'.54—dc20   95-25785

$\mathscr{A}$ mother's memories, like lustrous pearls strung one by one, become her treasures. From the birth of her child to the birth of her child's child, these memories are her most cherished possession.

Here are those precious moments from a mother's life put into words . . . and tributes from the children who "rise up and call her blessed"!

Contents

A
Mother's
Memories

A Perfect Fit

You were so little,
　　Standing there
Enveloped
In your father's coat and hat,
The tie touching your toes . . .
"Look," you said,
A smile on your small face . . .
"I'm like Daddy!"

O yes, my son,
You are!
You've grown
Into his clothes,
And you've
Taken on his tender ways . . .
For as a child
You wore
More than his coat and hat . . .

You were enveloped
In his love.

My Son, the Graduate

Go west, young man, go west . . .
Like Duke Wayne
You will sit tall in the saddle
As you ride to take the sunset.

Success is yours,
And we send you to it . . .
Bravely, brightly,
With rightly arranged smiles
On our faces,
Looking at you
With the love and logic
That tells us you are
Wise and wonderful
And grown in grace
And ready, O yes,
Ready!

And so you go
Galloping toward life
As we stand
Waving wildly,
Shouting our good-byes . . .

While hid behind my heart
There is the sad, insistent
Whisper . . .
Come back, young man, come back.

Where God Is

I want
To touch You, Lord . . .
I know
You're there
But sometimes
I need
    Something tangible. . . .
    Something I can hold to, cling to,
    Something I can put my arms around,
    Something I can *see*.

Then go, Daughter . . .
    Find a child
    Who needs tears wiped away,
    Hurts kissed and made well,
    Fears calmed.
Touch the child
And you will touch Me. . .

For inasmuch as you have
Put your arms around
One of the least of these
You have also
Held Me.

Sunday School

The children's class
Had constructed carefully
A cardboard Noah's ark,
And plastic animals
Were patiently lined up
Two by two
For a cruise of
Forty days and forty nights.

Then the class was taken
To the sanctuary
For the sermon.

Midway through
His timely dissertation
The preacher raised his voice
In fine oratorical form . . .

"And what, I ask you,
What
Will clean up this old world?"

John William, age four,
Leaned over to his teacher
And whispered solemnly . . .
"A soapy flood would do it."

Oh, if only it were
So simple.

Remember?

Was ever a wedding
So wonderful
As hers?

The day my daughter married . . .
The music of Mendelssohn,
Cascades of color,
Orchids and lilies
And lavender organdy,
Candlelight catching on
Satin and lace and lashes
Wet with tears . . .

But more,
More than all that,
There was such wonder,
Such awe, such magic,
As love walked down that aisle!

Was ever a wedding
So wonderful
as hers?

Once . . .
There was mine.

A

Grandmother's

Memories

Cherub in Disguise

O child of my child . . .
What do you dream
As you drift
On your cloud of sleep?

Do you laugh
With the littlest angels
As you hide-and-seek
Among the stars?

Do you swing
On the pearly gates
And splash
In puddles of soft, silvery dew?

Do you play your harp
And sing the songs of your tiny soul?

From His glory you came,
And to His glory you will return . . .
But in between you're *here*
For as long as you live on earth . . .

To bring a bit of
Heaven to our
Home!

The Composers

ear Lord . . .

Little Anna lay in my arms,
One week old and wonderful,
And suddenly I wanted
To sing!
No matter that
I can't carry a tune
Or hold a note
Or harmonize . . .
There was music
In me . . .
Music!

This must be what it means
To have a
Song in my heart.

O let's don't stop with
A song, Lord . . .
Let's do a
Symphony!

Little Love

n pink polka dots
She stood pensive
By her bed
And hugged her bunny
To herself.
Lightly she laid
A soft cheek on his head,
And with a tiny hand
She patted his back.

It was exactly as *she*
Had been held only
Moments before.
Exactly as *she* had been
Patted and petted . . .
This baby,
Just barely beginning to
Walk and to talk,
Had yet so easily
Learned love.

Obviously
You're never too young
For love lessons!

Rubies, Ribbons,
and Bows

Her tiny tiara
Toppled to one side
As she waved to her second-grade subjects . . .
She was seven,
Queen of the masquerade . . .
In royal parade around the school courtyard,
Her throne a golf cart covered with
Crepe paper streamers,
Ribbons, and bows.

That night at supper
Under gentle supervision
She made the salad and set the table,
Bathed her small brother's hands and face,
And emptied the kitty-litter box.

She is learning
That a queen also serves . . .
And a virtuous woman
Looks well to the ways of her household . . .
Weaving, working,
Spinning the spiritual fabric of her home,
For then is she
Truly valuable . . .

Far above
   Rubies,
   Ribbons,
   Bows!

God's Child

At ten years
Her tiny shoulders were too small
To bear the burdens of the world . . .
But she tried!

When Angela and Amy
Refused to play the game together
She pulled them from the separate sides
Of the room . . .
"Please kiss and make up!"
She pleaded.

When John William
Spilled his fingerpaints
And left in a temper,
She followed him . . .
"At least you made a picture,"
She soothed.

When on Picnic day
It rained and the class
Sat gloomily inside
With their sandwiches,
She walked to the window . . .
"But the flowers look delighted,"
She observed.

34

I watched,
Remembering . . .
Blessed are the peacemakers,
   For they shall be called
   The children of God.

Landscapes

There are twenty years
Between the two . . .
My child
And my child's child.

Twenty years between two children
Who are the dear
Delight of my life . . .
My pleasure
My treasure
My love . . .
Each child the same!

But in *me* a miracle occurred . . .
A metamorphosis!
I am no longer 'Mother'
With a thousand things to sort . . .
With hurried, worried, weary days and nights,
Sometimes losing sight of love
In the avalanche of meals, manners, measles,
Costumes for the Christmas pageant
And sudden adolescence . . .
I am "Grandmother"!

I hug without hurry.
I talk.
She listens.
I spin old-time tales
Like long threads linking
Our lives
Generation to generation.
I rest.
The large, looming mountain
Of responsibility is moved . . .

And I can see the scenery
Of love.

Who Loves You?

$\mathcal{I}$ saw him
Running toward me,
The son of my son,
Four years old and flying . . .
"Look at me, Grandmudder!
   I'm a bird
   I'm a plane
   I'm Superman!"

He climbed the ladder
To the top of the slide
Balancing briefly . . .
"Look at me, Grandmudder!"
   As he skidded headlong
   Down the silver slope.

He tumbled topsy-turvy
Into the pool
Sputtering,
His arms spinning in wide cartwheels . . .
"Look at me, Grandmudder!
   I'm a motoboat!"

O son of my son,
Who loves you, Baby?

"Grandmudder!"

Stages of Life

I've played lots of roles
In my day,
But these two have
Been the longest . . .
Mother and
Grandmother . . .

Seems I've signed a
Lifetime contract
And I'm still
On stage!

Through the years
The scripts changed,
Rehearsals were long,
Lines were hard to learn.
Sometimes performances came
Before I was ready,
And often for
An audience of one . . .
One child
Who needed my time, attention, love
Discipline. . . .
And no matter how well I did
There was no thunderous applause . . .
Just many hugs and kisses
And sticky Valentines
And once a tinsel halo
For my hair.

I was never a noble heroine,
Madame Curie, Queen Esther, Joan of Arc,
But I've loved every part I've played . . .

And I've been happy
With my stages.

To Mom,

with

Love

No More Tears

When I was small
My mother had two simple solutions
To everything . . .
Cinnamon tea and
Bubble baths.
There was no problem which
Could not be solved
With one or the other.

If it was winter
And things went wrong,
We had a cup of tea.
If it was summer
And I had a sad day
She'd say, "Let's have a bubble bath."
And as the frothy foam rose around me
She'd sing . . .
"Bubble, bubble, *double* bubble,
Take away my toil and trouble" . . .
And soon my tears would be
Forgotten.

Often, then, she'd tell me . . .
"In heaven there's a shining river,
And when we have crossed *those* waters,
God will take away our tears
Forever."
It sounded wondrous to me then,
And it sounds wondrous
To me now.

It's been half a century
Since my childhood,
But I still resort to bubble baths
On sad days . . .
And as the turmoil of my mind
Melts away I think . . .
If a simple bubble bath can bring
This much comfort,

I can't wait to wade in those
Wondrous waters
Where my tears will be *forever*
Forgotten.

How heavenly!

Myself

She told me
I was talented . . .
Witty, wise,
Wonderful . . .
The best, most beautiful
Child in the world.

She was wrong,
Of course . . .
I know how ordinary I am.

But somewhere inside
This ordinary mind and body
Is the most
Extraordinary self . . .
     Worthy always,
     Even wonderful . . .

Because my mother
Said so!

With All My Heart

It's Mother's Day again,
And I've bought the card . . .
But how should I
Sign it . . .
What should I say?

Should I remind her
Of the nights she
Stayed awake, watching,
Or the days she spent
In prayer?
Should I reminisce
About the clothes she sewed
When we were too poor for
Store bought,
Or the countless
Birthday cakes,
The chocolate cookies,
The pot roasts and potatoes every Sunday?
Should I remember
How she made sacrifices for me
As willingly as she made beds,
Shined my shoes,
Patched and repatched worn out
Knees and elbows in my
Sweaters, jeans, and sweatpants?
Should I recall
How she led me to love
The Lord,
To claim his promises,
To keep his commandments?
How should I sign this card . . .
What should I say?

WAIT! I KNOW!

  Thank you, Mom . . .
  With all my heart,
  I love you!

The Conspirators

They planned it together,
My mother and God . . .
How I would marry
Just the right man
For me!

They talked it over
For years . . .
The qualities he would have
The quiet strength
The Christian character
The LOVE
Even the light
In his eyes . . .
And then, leaving nothing
To chance,
They described him
To me . . .
"Mr. Marvelous."

With such clear guidelines
To follow
I *found* him!

The conspirators were
Not surprised . . .
After all, it was
Their plan . . .

And I have been thankful
To both of them
Ever since!

Mother's Husband

I was always
"Daddy's girl."
We shared a love of
Music and mischief,
And we read books to one another,
Sitting under the Mississippi pines
On Saturday mornings.

I was nine years old when we read
Gone With the Wind.
I knew I'd never be
As pretty as Scarlett . . .
But Daddy said I had more sense.

He borrowed money
To give me the wedding I wanted . . .
And later drove through
Hail and high water, literally,
To see my firstborn.

That's another thing
Mother did for me . . .

She chose Daddy.

Hope for the Heart

always think of Mother
When the redbuds bloom . . .
It was her sign,
Her signal from the Lord
That life was
Looking up!
"The redbuds have bloomed,"
She'd say exultantly.
"Soon we can sit outside!"

Sometimes she sent pictures
Of the redbuds blooming
In her backyard . . .
It was a faithful affirmation
To her
That God was in
His heaven,
And all was right in the world . . .
"You can rely on spring," she'd say.

Then there was the bitter cold winter
When she lay so sick
And we watched the forbidding weather
From her hospital room . . .
"Don't worry," she whispered,
"I'll be home before the
Redbuds bloom. . . ."
And she was.

Today in the park
The redbuds were blooming!
I think the Lord and Mother
Must be sitting outside . . .
I certainly am.
Of all the things she taught me
To look for in life,
Perhaps the best
Was spring . . .

And its precious
Promises!

A Red Rose

*I*t was Mother's Day . . .
And as we left the little church
There were by the door two baskets . . .
One of red roses, one of white,
A gift for each worshiper . . .
A red rose for those
Whose mothers were living,
And white for those
Whose mothers were not.

I stood beside the white roses . . .
For my mother had been
In heaven for many years . . .
But suddenly I reached
Into the other basket
And took a red rose.

She is more real to me
Now than ever, I thought . . .
Each time I give my love,
Guide my children,
Guard my values,
Instinctively touch
My husband's heart . . .
I remember Mother!
She taught me,
Led me,
Shaped my life.
So lovingly!
Her memory lives . . .

And my rose is red.